Emergency

Sue Graves

Nelson

Contents

Getting Help	**4**
The Police Service	**6**
Cars and Helicopters	8
Boats and Horses	9
The Ambulance Service	**10**
The Ambulance	12
The Ambulance Crew	13
The Fire Service	**14**
The Fire Engine	16
The Fire-fighters	17
Keeping Safe from Fire	18
The Coastguard	**20**
Keeping Safe at the Seaside	22
Warning Flags	23
Glossary	**24**

Getting Help

Sometimes people need help.

They may be ill, or they may be in danger.

When people need help like this, it is called an emergency. You can call one of these services for help.

The Police Service

The Ambulance Service

The Fire Service

The Coastguard

To get help from one of these services, you must dial 999.

An operator will answer your 999 call. He or she will ask you which service you need.

The operator uses a computer screen to deal with your call.

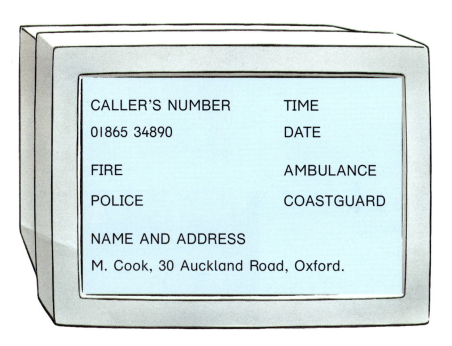

The operator will connect you to the emergency service you need. The emergency service will ask you:
- *what* the trouble is
- *where* the trouble is
- *where* you are calling from
- *what* your name is.

The Police Service

Sometimes, people need the police to help them. The police help people in lots of ways.

Call the police if a crime has taken place.

Call the police if people are in danger.

Bomb scare

Gas leak

Call the police if there has been a traffic accident.

In a traffic accident, the police find out if anyone is hurt.

They find out what happened.

The police make sure the road is safe for other motorists to use.

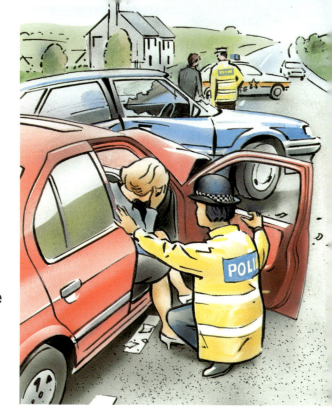

Cars and Helicopters

Police use different types of transport.

This police officer drives a fast car.

This police officer rides a motorbike.

This police officer flies a helicopter. He can spot a traffic jam or a suspect from a helicopter.

Boats and Horses

Mounted police officers ride horses. They help to control large crowds of people.

The river police patrol the rivers.

The river police use boats like this.

The Ambulance Service

When people become ill suddenly, they need an ambulance to take them to hospital quickly.

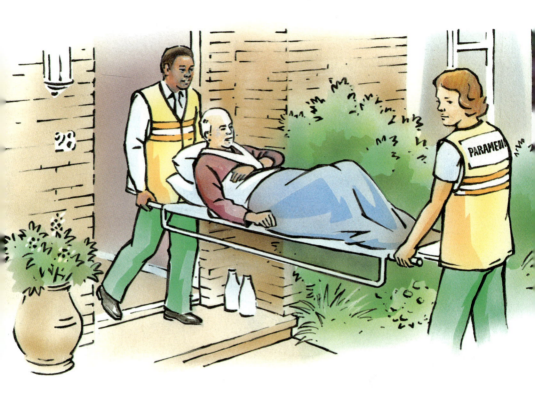

When people have bad accidents, they need an ambulance to take them to hospital quickly, too.

An ambulance has to get to a patient quickly.

The blue flashing light and loud siren warn people that an ambulance is trying to get through the traffic.

When drivers hear the siren, they should pull over and stop to let the ambulance pass.

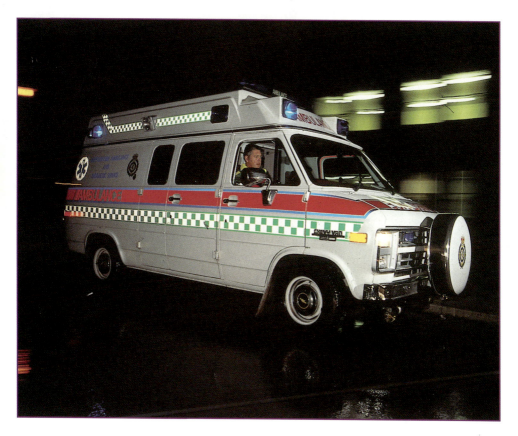

The Ambulance

The inside of an ambulance is like a small hospital. It has life-saving equipment in it.

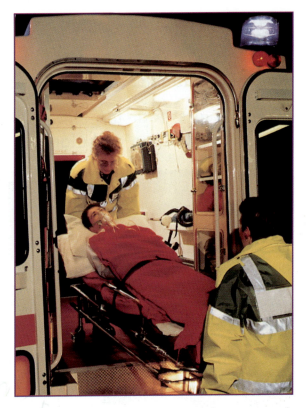

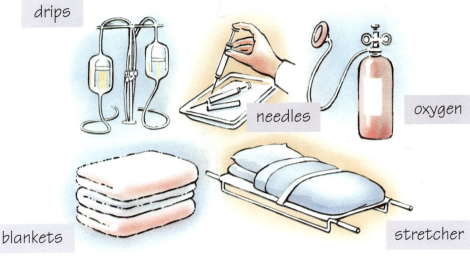

drips

needles

oxygen

blankets

stretcher

The Ambulance Crew

An ambulance crew is trained to stabilise patients as quickly as possible. To stabilise a patient means to make them as calm and safe as possible for the trip to a hospital. An ambulance crew uses the life-saving equipment in the ambulance to stabilise the patients.

The patient is then taken to hospital for treatment.

An ambulance crew

The Fire Service

The Fire Service helps in many different ways. The people in the Fire Service are called fire-fighters. They put out fires in all kinds of places.

Fire-fighters can put out a fire in a factory, a forest, a car, a house, a plane, a ship and even a chip pan.

Fire-fighters also help to rescue people from floods.
They pump the floodwater out from people's homes.

Fire-fighters help to cut people out of cars in bad accidents.

Fire-fighters rescue animals too.

The Fire Engine

The fire engine has lots of equipment on it to help the firefighters deal with any emergency.

It has lots of tools.

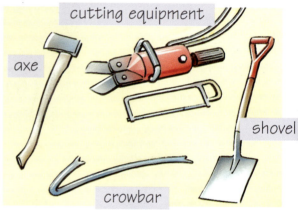

It also has a water tank filled with 1800 litres of water. If more water is needed, the fire fighters connect the hose to a hydrant. A hydrant is like a large tap in the street.

The Fire-fighters

The fire-fighters wear a special uniform. The uniform helps to protect them from danger.

A fire-fighter wears a uniform like this.

- helmet
- jacket
- torch
- gloves
- trousers
- steel-capped boots

Fire-fighters put on breathing apparatus, when they go into a smoke-filled building.

Breathing apparatus

Keeping Safe from Fire

A fire at home can start for lots of reasons.

It can start because someone has been careless or silly.

Playing with matches can start a fire.

Leaving toys or clothes too near a heater can start a fire.

Forgetting to unplug things can start a fire.

A smoke alarm can keep you safe from fire, too. It warns you if there is a fire in your home.

A smoke alarm

If there is a fire in your home, you must:

- **GET OUT**
- **STAY OUT**
- **CALL 999**

You and your family should make an escape plan in case of fire.

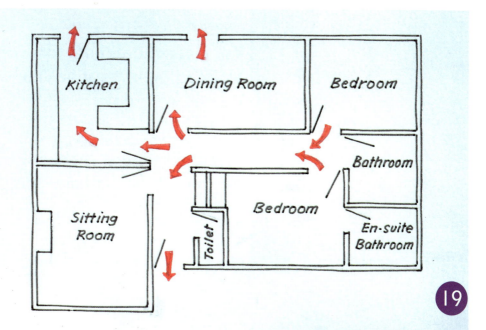

The Coastguard

When people need help at the seaside, the Coastguard rescue them.

The Coastguard use boats and helicopters to rescue people.

The Coastguard rescue people from boats and they rescue people from airbeds.

lifeboat

dinghy

helicopter

They rescue people who are trapped on cliffs, and those people who have been cut off by the tide.

The Coastguard rescue swimmers and divers, too.

The Coastguard also rescue people who may be in danger out at sea.

The Coastguard rescue ships and tankers.

The Coastguard can also fight fire on other ships.

The Coastguard rescue fishing boats.

Keeping Safe at the Seaside

Remember:

1 Always tell someone where you are going.

2 Don't climb on the cliffs.

3 Never swim just after a meal.

4 Don't take airbeds onto the sea.

5 Don't play on the rocks.

6 Watch the tide.

Warning Flags

If you do swim in the sea, look out for these warning flags.

Red flag means danger. Do not swim.

A yellow flag means be careful. Strong swimmers only.

A green flag means the sea is calm.

You can swim between these flags. A lifeguard patrols here.

You cannot swim between these flags. Windsurfers and surfers only.

Glossary

accident – something bad that happens by chance

crime – an act that is against the law

divers – people who wear special equipment to go to the bottom of the sea

equipment – kit that helps you do a job

factory – a building where goods are made by machines

lifeguard – someone who helps to rescue people from drowning

patient – a person who is getting medical care

suspect – a person who is believed to have committed a crime

tankers – large ships that carry liquid goods, such as oil

tide – the movement of the sea coming into the land and then going away again

transport – means of getting from one place to another

windsurfers – people who stand on special sailing boards to sail across the water